The Race

Within

Tarus Crayton

Copyright ©2020 Tarus Crayton

All rights reserved. No part of this publication may be reproduced, distributed, or transmitted in any form or by any means, including photocopying, recording, or other electronic or mechanical methods, without the prior written permission of the publisher, except in the case of brief quotations embodied in critical reviews and certain other noncommercial uses permitted by copyright law.

ISBN-978-1-951300-77-7

Liberation's Publishing – West Point - Mississippi

Dedication

This book is dedicated to
Teri, Jaron, Makayla and Kylan

Embrace your uniqueness, talents, and gifts to write your own narrative even when others insist on developing your plot.

The Race Within

Table of Content

Introduction 7

    Chapter One: The Pacesetter 9

    Chapter Two: Runner's Interference 37

    Chapter Three: Mastering the Curve 61

    Chapter Four: The Straight away 69

    Chapter Five: Anchored Through Experience . 79

Epilogue/Conclusion 99

Acknowledgement 101

About The Author 103

Introduction

Congratulations on your purchase of *The Race Within*. This book is about some of the physical and spiritual hardships that life may present, and how the average person can overcome these challenges with the help of God. If you are struggling with life issues, this book shows that a person doesn't have to fit in society's neatly wrapped box for the power of God to move in his or her life. God's only requirement is to confess with a repentant heart and be receptive to his leading.

This book will teach you purpose does exist in pain. From childhood to now, God delivered me through circumstances to help others find their strength in Him. Whenever you are spiritually dehydrated, God desires to be the well that fills you. This book will encourage honest dialogue amongst you, family members, and God. It requires asking the hard questions to grow. While writing this book, it provided a source of healing for me. Hopefully, as you read this book healing will occur for you. Don't just read the book. Digest it. It will change your life.

The Race Within

Chapter One: The Pacesetter

Adopt the pace of nature; her secret is patience – Ralph W. Emerson

Focus! I say to myself as sweat the size of pearls trickle down my face and fall to the ground. *Find your pace. Keep going! Are you serious?* I instinctively gaze into the horizon picturing the hidden difficulties on this never-ending course. *I've never run this route before. Stay calm. Take a deep breath.* Just at that moment, I glance ahead, a hill – no, a massive mountain quietly displays itself before me.

This is hard. In fact, it is more challenging than I ever anticipated. Without warning, my knees begin to buckle underneath me. I nose-dive to the uncompromising ground. The amount of energy this race requires leaves me questioning my endurance. *Perhaps, I've bitten off more than I can chew. I don't think that I can do this.* As a matter of fact, my desire to finish this race declines by the minute. Comparing myself to others is futile. While scanning the area, better conditioned figures rush past me like powerful deer in the middle of hunting season. *What am I doing wrong? I must have been out of my mind to compete.* Yet, a voice distinctly *whispers,* ***"run with endurance the race that is set before you." Hebrews 12:1 (KJV)*** Lord knows I'm trying, but perception politely informs me that danger is present.

Everyone knows training for any race presents challenges. The physical discomfort of running is only one fraction of difficulty. The wind is another. Learning to adapt to the wind as the seasons change is the key to any run. Oftentimes, this inability to adapt and the mental clarity to run another day prevents many amateurs from becoming masters. One mile today. Four tomorrow. My attention shifts to my trainer Ulysses as he explains his expectations to me. His strong countenance says he is a warrior, and his chiseled frame confirms it. Knowingly, I am in the presence of a champion. Inwardly though, I can't help but roll my eyes upward as he offers a rigorous training plan to guide me along the way. Though his determination is etched in his face, my fortitude is not as engraved.

Passionately Ulysses says, "You'll develop endurance if you don't quit. Uncertainty lingers silently in the heart of every man waiting to show itself strong. That's why we must ***"hide ourselves for a little while to determine our true self" Isaiah 26:20)KJV*** so we do not succumb to doubt. When you set unrealistic or unattainable goals for yourself, you slowly suffocate personal growth. Remember, the champion isn't always the person who wins, but it is the person who perseveres."

I nod in agreement, somewhat listening and somewhat agitated, getting lost as my thoughts float to the upcoming races. Instinctively, I shift the weight of my body from left to right and clasp my hands tightly together.

"Visualize not only the main course but every route in between. Even when you experience pain along the way, continue to pour into others."

"But," I attempt to interrupt him.

He clears his throat and says, "Pain lasts as long as you focus on it. When others become your priority, the pain disappears, and true healing begins. Life is a marathon not a sprint. And to truly win, you must lose pieces of yourself to gain wisdom. Did I answer your question?"

"Yes sir."

After training with Ulysses for several weeks, I understood the advice given to me. Some days, my hard work proudly displayed the conclusions of these most challenging efforts, and other days, I simply had to trust the process. Today is one of those days. I could have watched the race from the sidelines, but a part of me yearns to validate myself. Probably because people's perceptions often dictate expectations. According to my friends, competing in the race was an absolute necessity for me. Sometimes, though, listening to others is a welcome diversion but acting on their advice leads to self-destruction.

For some competitors, finding the courage to begin a race and the sustainability to finish often proves difficult. Perhaps, physical races personify journeys of tangible and intangible threats all creation must confront. During my first run, the squirrels frolicked securely in their familiar habitat. Without warning, I emerged as an imminent threat jeopardizing their peace. The noise of my heavy breathing startled them and triggered a survival reaction. Isn't it unusual how the perception of noise behaves as a powerful weapon to initiate a fight or flight response within us? From then on, my understanding of the dangers of noise grew. Even though I didn't always operate in silence, I knew it contained great strength.

On every occasion that I have stumbled or fallen, internal noise propositioned me to desert my endeavors. Even though my grandma is gone, her soothing voice of encouragement neutralized the internal noise. "*Honey*, this too shall pass if you just focus on your keeper. *God makes everything possible.*" **Matthew 19:6** Whenever our "spirits felt burdened", Grammy sensed our sadness and offered support.

She was deeply devoted to God and always willing to do his work. In fact, each Sunday, Grammy and her best friends, Bessie Mae and Eunice, gathered at the third pew to worship the Lord by making a joyful noise. Truthfully, none of the ladies carried a tune well, but when their voices blended with the choir, the music sounded heavenly. Usually after two songs, Grammy and her friends became overwhelmed by the presence of the Holy Ghost! As a child, my friends and I were often frightened when the Holy Ghost came. I guess because we didn't fully understand Him. When He visited, people moved around sporadically and uncontrollably. At times, some cried hysterically, and others screamed loudly while running around the church. As children, we didn't know what to think.

When Grammy and her friends became overwhelmed by His presence, they belted out high pitched hallelujahs, flailed their arms wildly, and fell backwards onto the pew. We thought the falling backwards was more from exhaustion than His presence.

One time, Ms. Eunice became so overwhelmed in the presence that her wig flew two pews backwards. As children, we hid under the pew until these episodes were over, and the preacher began the introduction to his sermon. To us, it seemed as if he presented the same sermon which lasted for hours each Sunday. In retrospect, even though lives were being impacted, the impression given to us as children was one of indifference. The sermon length and complexity didn't exactly wet our palate.

Grammy's advice never failed me. But right now, as I lay in a state of paralysis from my fall, questions about my faith invade my thoughts. *I've never questioned Grammy's advice before.* Is my faith weakening? Grammy said Jesus took our sorrows on the cross and his burden is light. However, I can't help but think, if he took them, then why does my spirit feel so heavy? Besides, the crushing reality is that Grammy's in Heaven. When she died, my soul fainted. I cried day and night from the emptiness that occupies my heart. The loss of Grammy happened all at once, but the reality of the loss occurred in tiny pieces. Each morning I woke to greet her, death's sting struck me repeatedly. As grief tried to take residency in my heart, I pleaded for strength. *Why did death make the scars so deep?* The faint roar of the crowd invades my sanctity of peace at this moment. The voices act to persuade me, but the one coaching me to give up whispers louder. *I could just lay here. What's the point in enduring anyway?* Yet, I will not and cannot fall victim to the devil's devices.

Superficially, this symbiotic competition offered a way to showcase my athletic prowess while exposing a conscious revelation of inner strength. The subject of discovery, of course, is me. I am unique. Teri Olivia Davis. The good girl. The smart and dependable one. The over achiever. The predictable one, and the one who never takes chances, especially on herself. Most amazingly, people characterize me as intimidating, dogmatic, and even guarded – until they get to know me.

To really understand me though, you need insight into my childhood. Various imaginations exist in the mind of a child, and I of course was no different. Perhaps my biggest imagination is that children deserve love. The idea of what that love feels like varies for everyone. Certainly, when it's given, it is felt. As a preteen, my family teased me about the size of my nose and my breasts. They insisted my nose didn't fit my face. However, I embrace the fact that my nose is you know, unique.

On one occasion, Momma declared, "Girl, your breasts are huge! They just poke out all over the place." Her criticism stung. Partly because I wanted her approval.

Sometimes, though, I think momma didn't like me very much. Oftentimes, she was very critical of me particularly during my pubescent years. Even though my body matured, I wasn't fully aware of the physical changes taking place. I had breasts. Since my frame is petite, my breasts appeared larger than normal. This upset me because of the unwanted attention.

Momma's statements made me feel defective in some way and super self-conscious. So, in order to not bring attention to myself or my developing breasts, I hunched my back to draw my boobs inward. In fact, momma's critique had a lingering effect on me. I disliked my body. As an adult, I would wear a minimizer bra to make my boobs appear smaller until I was well in my thirties.

Puberty is a confusing time for most everyone; it is a time of change, and at twelve years of age, the superficial narrative for my life reflected nothing but disorder. Grammy frequently said something about *when I was in Christ, I would become a new creature and old things would pass away. 2 Corinthians* **5:17** Years passed before I became that new creature Grammy talked about, and all these changes molded me in the creation.

My grandparents, Pop and Grammy, reared me, and because of them, I felt safe and secure. They didn't shower me with a lot of material things; in fact, we didn't have much of anything. What we did have was lots of love. For every time Grammy cooked my meals, read me a story, or just talked to me, the compassion in her heart spoke to me. When Grammy died, Pop picked up where she left off. Plenty of times, he gave my brother and me one dollar of his hard-earned money and took us to the Jitney Jungle. We could spend it on whatever we desired. To me, that was love. Not because of the material value associated with their actions but because of the sacrifices they made for us.

However, the relationship that I have with my mother and father is completely different. My father abandoned me before I was even born. Even though

I know my mom and lived in the same house with her for a number of years, she lived her life to the fullest, and that living didn't include any of her children. Except my brother, and that's another story within itself. During my formative years, I rarely saw her, and when I did, pleasant didn't describe the experience.

Nevertheless, life is an echo. All that a person gives, returns. How we make it through this competition determines an individual's level of success, right? So many times, emotions create certain expectations within me, and this happens to be one of those times. For each moment I am in transition, I see myself. Christian. Woman. Black.

As a child, learning excited me. More often than not, I sat in a corner and read all day. As I thumbed through the pages, the words on the book came alive. Because we didn't have a lot of money, we didn't vacation like many of my friends. I had my books. With my books, I traveled anywhere in the world I desired and became whatever my heart could imagine. Reading and writing provided an escape for me; playing school became my therapy. Often, my cousins and I gathered my aunt's old magazines as classroom materials. Even in youth, I recognized the power of teaching. While pretending to instruct my class, confidence flowed through my veins.

English became my favorite subject to teach. Not only did reading the written word take my imagination to another level, but learning the history of the English language, conjugating verbs, and writing was like an aphrodisiac. Also, my passion for vocabulary words became my focus, and fortunately or unfortunately, depending on how you look at it, I learned many new vocabulary words and definitions early in life.

When I was five years old, I attended an educational program called head start. This program provided an "early" start in learning for financially challenged families. One afternoon after Mr. Rogers dismissed school, he told me I was going to my momma's new house. Before, I had lived with my Aunt Rachel. The head start bus driver drove me to my mom's new house and dropped me off.

My mom greeted me as I jumped off the bus. She took me inside and I examined every inch of the house. Being in my mom's house was a lot different than Aunt Rachel's house. Not only from a physical standpoint but mentally as well. Light gray brick covered the frame of the house. Instead of green grass, red clay covered the yard. No familiar smells permeated the atmosphere like at Aunt Rachel's house, but I learned to adapt. It was here, in my momma's house, that my education intensified through life experiences and my knowledge of vocabulary words grew more often than I preferred.

During the summers, Grammy and Pop kept all seven of their grandkids at my mom's house until my momma and her sisters finished work. My cousin Sophie, who is a year older than me, and I spent most of our time together. We often laid at the foot of the bed in my momma's room to watch television. I'm not really sure when Sophie learned this new skill or what it was for that matter, but on one particular day, she decided to demonstrate what she had learned. As we sat in my momma's room, Sophie leaned over and kissed me on the lips. I had seen this done a couple of times on television, but we were not permitted to watch this kind of "entertainment". Whenever Sophie came over, she wanted to practice kissing; so, we sat in the dark, the television light illuminating the room, and practiced kissing. One day, Sophie decided to show me some other "stuff" she had learned. I didn't know what to call it, how to pronounce it, or even spell it, but I knew it wasn't something that I wanted to keep doing.

I felt dirty and ashamed afterwards. A piece of my innocence fled, and the sparkle in my eyes dimmed a little. Many years later, I discovered that the word was molestation.

The *enemy comes to kill, steal, and destroy, **John 10:10*** and after reflecting upon the challenges in my life, I can agree. The experience with Sophie altered my interactions with others forever. Consequently, I never wanted to be left alone with her or my Aunt Jezzie. I didn't want to visit Aunt Jezzie's house. Something about her scared me. But she didn't scare me physically. Her spirit frightened me because I never felt safe around her. Not only did I have uneasy feelings about Aunt Jezzie, but the sensation was even stronger around Uncle Aaron.

Uncle Aaron went out of his way to make me comfortable. Whenever he came around, he brought my brother and I candy and wanted me to sit on his lap, but my "feeler" said stay away from him. *Why did I feel like that? Adults are good people, and family won't hurt you!* Maybe this is where my cousin Sophie learned the new things that she showed me. In any case, I didn't want the opportunity to learn any more "stuff" from their family. I'll just take my chances and figure it out on my own.

One weekend, Uncle Aaron wanted my brother and me to spend the night at their house. I was very reluctant, but they had a dog! Everyone knew that I liked dogs. It was a Great Dane named Bella. Great Danes aren't exactly my favorite breed; nevertheless, all dogs need love! The best part was that this Great Dane could do tricks! My eyes widened with amazement after seeing Bella shake a person's hand. The unknown dangers escaped me because Bella's playfulness was so enticing.

No temptations have come over us that we couldn't defeat, but Bella's seemingly simplicity and purity lured me from safety. *1 Corinthians 10:13* Even though my "sight" remained intact, my faith was being tested, and I succumbed to the pleasure.

Therefore, my brother and I packed some clothes to spend the night with my Aunt Jezzie. The house was nice. It was bigger than my mom's house, and it had a well-manicured yard. Aunt Jezzie and Uncle Aaron had the best of the best. They had all the newest appliances and two fancy cars. Being over there was like something in a movie or a scene from the old tv show, the Jeffersons.

Obviously, they had "moved on up" from the rest of our family and Aunt Jezzie's course to prosperity only allowed her to occasionally remind momma and Aunt Rachel of her affluence. Aunt Jezzie and her children only wore designer clothes and had the best of the best. As I looked around the house, loose change lay everywhere. I remember thinking that they were rich! Especially since everywhere I looked, I could find at least seventy-five cents just lying around. That was some major money to me! Though I was tempted to put a couple of seventy-five cents in my pocket, I never did.

My cousins, my brother, and I played outside until the sun went down. It was different playing over there. At home, we made toys to play with. At Aunt Jezzie's, the toys were already assembled! How could any child not like this? By the time my Aunt Jezzie called us into the house to get ready for bed, my uneasiness had started to diminish a little.

Maybe I had been overreacting! Aunt Jezzie ran our bath water and gave us towels to wash up for the night. They had a rule that you couldn't lock the door to the bathroom when you took a bath. *No problem I thought. It's actually not so bad over here.* I went into the bathroom to take my bath first.

One by one, I peeled off my shirt: my shorts and underpants followed. I unfastened my bra, (even though I only had enough for a training bra at the time) and threw it onto the floor. I placed the shower cap on my head and relaxed in the tub. This wasn't just an ordinary bath! It was a bubble bath, and I enjoyed it to the fullest. I stayed in their tub until my skin turned into what looked like a soft crumpled prune. Finally, I decided that it was time to get out of the tub, and just at that moment, the door creaked open.

Tomorrow couldn't come soon enough. That night, fear kept me from sleep, and darkness unhurriedly became daylight.

The next day, my brother and I traveled home, and I could finally feel a sense of relief. Momma and Aunt Rachel didn't say anything on the car ride home, but they sensed that I didn't enjoy my time at Aunt Jezzie's house. My "feelers" demanded that I avoid that place, and after the visit, that's exactly what I did. *Maybe I should listen to them more often?*

Eventually, I discovered that my "feelers" were God's spiritual gift to me. Before, I understood nothing about spiritual gifts, only regular gifts! I was grateful whenever I received a regular gift because we rarely got gifts. Momma usually spent her money on cigarettes, beer, and the casino. Most times, momma came back from the casino angry because she usually lost her bill money. Pop mowed extra lawns to help momma with the bills. *When God gives you a gift, you are special.* Therefore, I was extremely grateful to get a gift from God.

The chants of the crowd become stronger and stronger. Someone yells *Get up! Get up, you may have fallen, but you can do this. Stand firm. No fear. Love. Power. And Self-Discipline. You are victorious!* I chuckle. *At this point, does victory live in me? Am I imitating the life of an imposter?* For many imposters have gone out into the world and labored in vain. **2 John 1:7** As I contemplate getting up, the only thought that comes to mind is *how much will I do to be accepted? Is it worth it?* Trying to prove worthy of another's acceptance is very costly.

I've never been the "typical" child. For some reason, God saw fit to give me a measure of intelligence, and I could always "see" and "feel" things that other people couldn't. I guess that's why the enemy attacked me. Years would pass before I met others who were like me. Grammy said that I was special, *fearfully and wonderfully made*. **Psalm 139:14** Somehow, I must learn to build self-trust. I guess God decided that I needed to work on this element in my life also. Hence, the different challenges that he has allowed me to face. It is during these times that I learned more words: faith, determination, and perseverance.

Throughout my life, I always wanted the experience of family. My concept of the family experience entailed having mom and dad under one roof. My friends' families embodied this family experience with two-parent homes, nice houses, nice cars, and most importantly, love. At least that is a person's perception from the outside. Only after graduating high school would I learn that my friends and I were living in houses made of the same material – glass. One only needs to shatter someone else's house before his or hers breaks. Doesn't that lessen the severity? Maybe life taught me early to deal with brokenness so that I could help put others back together.

Momma's life entices the greatest thrill-seeker.

Married twice, the years that I spent under her roof, she lived an exciting life. Understand though, Momma's faced many setbacks for the sake of love; she's wasted immeasurable energy searching for love and running from pain. Patty Mae Michaels, clever and most definitely a ride or die. It's just that if she didn't believe that you were worth riding for, she didn't. Unfortunately, her family wasn't necessarily exempt from this behavior, but occasionally, momma's generosity overflowed. She bought us new outfits to celebrate holidays. For Christmas, we received one gift that we really wanted.

The cabbage patch kid doll made its store debut in 1982, but it captivated my attention four years later in middle school! The life-like qualities of the dolls made every little girl want one, and sure enough, all of my friends' parents purchased them a cabbage patch kid doll when the dolls hit the shelves. Our fifth-grade teacher let the girls bring their dolls to school. I did not have one, so I felt left out. My sympathetic friends allowed me the opportunity to love on their baby-dolls throughout the day. Imagining each baby-doll was my very own, I held on to their "babies" tightly. However, Christmas was nearing, and my anticipation of seeing my cabbage patch kid doll neatly wrapped under the tree intensified. Early Christmas morning, my brother and I raced to open gifts.

Momma and Conner's daddy sat in the living room talking. Before we opened the gifts, Momma said, "Your brother's daddy bought him that stuff." She offered this as an explanation to compensate for Conner's seven gifts to my one. The quantity of gifts didn't matter to me. Momma cared enough to get me something, and sure enough, my one gift rested under the tree. One special gift. Ready to be opened. Wanting to savor the moment, I watched my brother rip open his presents as happiness filled the air; Conner received everything he asked for. Now, though, it was my turn. Nothing could make the day better except tearing open the box to my very own cabbage patch doll that I had waited for all year. Drum roll please. *Get ready! What will she look like? What color is her hair?* My heart pumped with excitement while little butterflies danced in my stomach; Conner kept nudging me to hurry up and open the box. My hands slashed through the wrapping paper without concern and turned the box so that I now could look face to face at the most beautiful baby ever!

My eyes did a doubletake to capture the

moment. When I looked again, my voice failed me, and I lowered my head so that no one saw the biggest teardrop cascade down my cheek. Peggy. Peggy the Pumpkin Patch kid. A knock off of the original. Don't get me wrong. The doll was beautiful, but it was not, and I repeat, was not a cabbage patch kid doll. When I glanced upward, laughter and merriment continued to fill the room, and no one noticed my disappointment. My heart genuinely felt happy for them. Yet, the gifting of Peggy caught me unawares, and I felt like an abbreviated piece of nothing.

Determined to make the best of my situation, I whispered a thank you to God for the gift and quickly escaped to my room. I placed Peggy on my side of the bed. Although Peggy wasn't a cabbage patch kid, she still deserved love and my affection. I resolved to love her; so, that's what I did.

Upon returning back to school after Christmas break, the teachers made us stand in front of the class to describe our Christmas holiday. *Oh, how I dreaded this!* My friends believed that Santa was bringing me a cabbage patch doll. Only problem is, he didn't come through. However, the more time I devoted to Peggy, the more I loved my pumpkin patch doll. Yet, part of me felt ashamed because she wasn't a cabbage patch doll. So, I only told my best friend that I had the pumpkin patch doll.

When I was twelve years old, momma's new boyfriend Buddy came to live with us. Buddy's lackluster appearance resembled the characters of the popular eighties sitcom Cheers. Nothing about him screamed show-stopping. In fact, Buddy was just ordinary, simple, and nice. Most all of our family liked Buddy except Pop. When it came to long-term relationships, Momma didn't have the best track record. Therefore, Pop regularly intervened when attitudes soured amongst momma and her boyfriends. Nevertheless, when Buddy came "home" from work, he brought Conner and me candy and other goodies. I inferred that I was his favorite since I received more goodies than my brother.

Every time one of momma's boyfriend came to live with us, the home atmosphere changed. She fixed hearty meals like fried pork chops with gravy and fluffy mashed potatoes on a regular basis, and she seemed happier. She talked more and became more sympathetic towards us. She cared for Buddy because she protected him while making sure he had most of what he wanted.

On Fridays, my older sister Tonia came home from college; she and my cousin Gigi were close. They did everything together. When Buddy met Tonia and Gigi for the first time, they laughed and chatted as if they had been old acquaintances. Momma felt they were all too friendly and was annoyed by their behavior. Consequently, she watched the interactions between them closely. In momma's mind, Tonia flirted with Buddy; therefore, she didn't hesitate to rebuke my sister for her actions. On Sundays, Tonia went back to college and life was business as usual around the house.

After momma cooked a good meal, she enjoyed taking a relaxing bath. She made me clean the tub and run her water along with washing dishes after everyone ate; my brother was too young. When momma took her bath, this presented an opportunity for Buddy to strike up a conversation in the kitchen with me while momma relaxed in the tub. This became our routine whenever momma took her bath. One day as I washed dishes, Buddy snuck into the kitchen and pinned me between the sink and him. He stood so close to me that I couldn't move, and I felt the sensation of moisture forming on my neck. He pressed something hard between the folds of my backside. Just as suddenly as he did it, we

The Race Within

heard momma shouting something from down the hall and he backed away. On several occasions, I had seen him stand close to momma like this, and she giggled uncontrollably. I felt weird though, a bit uncomfortable. Buddy didn't come in the kitchen to talk for a few days after that.

Momma started working later in the evenings. Many times, only Buddy, my brother, and I would be home until Pop finished mowing the lawns. Usually, my brother played with the neighbors and I stayed inside to read. Buddy regularly talked to me about books that I read, and in a playful manner, sometimes, he reached his hands out in an attempt to capture me. One day he accidentally touched my breasts. He apologized. When we played, he touched them accidentally a lot until one day it was not accidental anymore.

One Friday afternoon, momma worked later than usual. My comfort level diminished a lot being home alone with Buddy; however, Pop would arrive soon. Also, my brother was there. As I sat in the living room reading, Buddy and my brother were play wrestling. Soon after, my brother and I started tussling with each other, and before you know it, all three of us were wrestling. My brother went up front to get water, and he must have gone next door to play with the neighborhood children because only Buddy and me were left in the house.

Buddy and I were running all over the house playing tag and wrestling. Somehow, we ended up in my grandparents' room and he flung me on the bed. At first, I was giggling, trying to get from under his grip. Then, he repositioned himself, and I knew that this was no longer a game. *In fact, I felt danger. Immediate danger. The same feeling when my cousin showed me the "new" things she had learned!* He clamped his teeth onto my shirt and pinched my breasts as he aligned that familiar hardness on top of my private part. He started rocking on me and just as he did, we heard Pop's trailer come into the driveway. He hurriedly jumped up off me and neither one of us ever said a word. That weekend, my sister came home from college. Momma got into an argument with him and my sister; she said that they were having an inappropriate relationship. Of course, both of them denied it. And I was left with my thoughts.

As I lay in the sunken place, a still small voice almost like a whisper speaks to me. *Get up! Why are you here? Teri, why are you here?* I didn't know why I chose not to move. Well, maybe I did. I chose not to move because I felt defeated. Then a voice whispered, "You need only be still and know that I am God." **Psalms 46:10**

Life isn't exactly an episode of the *Cosby Show*. Somehow, my mind travels back to the five-point dominant buck -unrestricted, unbothered and confident while grazing on patches of vegetation. Without hesitation, the five-point runs away, and for the first time, an awakening rushes inside me. Anything is possible for the person who believes. **Mark 9:23** *Get up!* B*elieve! Failure is not trying!*

A sense of urgency develops within my soul. Unconsciously, I wipe the smudges of dirt off my blue Nike shorts and channel my vision to the present mission. The battle is in my mind. But my focus is on forgetting the past and straining towards my future. **Philipians 3:13**. I leap to my feet.

Facing forward, I began with a light gallop and then emerged into a full-fledged sprint. The adrenaline races through my veins while a thin coating of perspiration begins to cover my frame. The momentum from running so hard nearly thrust me face forward on the ground again. *At this speed, it won't take me long to get back in the race! Don't worry about the others. Just keep running! You got this. You. Got. This!* Using my peripheral vision, I catch a glimpse of some runners as the gap narrows. The breeze strikes my face and ruffles through my golden yellow tank top.

The Race Within

Chapter Two: Runner's Interference

I couldn't believe it! After a slight hiccup in starting the race, my entire body begins to cooperate for this competition. It's true that all things work together for good and according to purpose. **Romans 8:28** With each stride that I take, my body aches. Yet, none of that matters now. *Push past the pain.* I can finally see progress. I hear Grammy saying, *after you've suffered a while, the God of all grace will perfect, establish, strengthen, and settle you.* **1 Peter 5:10** It's weird how inspiration erupts from pain.

Finally, I relax in the groove as my thoughts drift to the warmth of a beautiful spring day. The melodious song of a pine warbler penetrates the stillness, and the sun rays gently strike my arms. Security settles in my spirit.

If you run long enough, change comes.

Twenty years ago, I met a man at work who would change my life forever. Marty Cook was seven years older than me, and at first, I didn't even notice him. He wasn't ruggedly handsome or overly muscular, rather big-boned and stout. As a matter of fact, anyone could see that he indulged in a few more brownies than he should have, but he looked strong. After a few sessions of small talk, Marty's disposition appeared pleasant enough, yet, with a subtle hint of deceit. He wasn't necessarily a prankster, but he was a good-time Charlie ready to pull someone's leg when summoned. My friend Rita was exactly the person to bring it out of him.

We all have those friends who are man crazy and tons of fun to be around, and Rita was no exception. She thought he was fine. However, she thought every man was fine and at times, some women too. Every time she saw him, she instantly morphed into flirtation mode or made some perverted gesture towards him. Since he wasn't romantically interested in Rita, he ignored her advances only to feed her a bone occasionally when he needed her.

Marty's eyes were fixated on me, and he made it known that I was the object of his attention. He pursued me like a lion hunting a gazelle; he used his best weapons to hunt me down and trap me. I felt like I was barking up the wrong tree entertaining Marty but reluctantly agreed to our first date. Actually, we grabbed a bite to eat at a local restaurant. My timidity kept me from going alone so Rita joined us. She ordered the chicken wings, and Marty and I both decided on steak. Rita enjoyed the chicken wings so much that she literally sucked the meat off of the bones in the restaurant.

After stuffing our faces, Rita and I left the restaurant because we had to go back to work. Consequently, her detective nature kicked in, and she suggested we scan the parking lot to determine what type of vehicle Marty drove. We didn't see a vehicle in the front of the parking lot that matched his character, so we drove to the back of the restaurant and spotted a red Nissan 240SX with a severely shattered windshield. Rita exited our car and determined that Marty's suspected windshield had been busted with a medium size brick. Before we could dive into a full-fledged conversation about the shattered windshield, Marty appeared. Rita started laughing uncontrollably indicating to him that it was time to spill the beans about what happened to the vehicle.

Since he wasn't forthcoming about the windshield, Rita asked him what happened to his car. He laughed and said we were better off not knowing. Eventually, he hesitantly confessed that his ex-wife was responsible for the shattered windshield. Though this entanglement with his ex-wife screamed problematic, I couldn't help feeling judgmental. Maybe he deserved a chance.

It wasn't long before I introduced Marty to my family. To them, our relationship resembled the epitome of perfection, and their expectation was marriage. Six months after we started dating, an event occurred that left me with a conflicting viewpoint of him. Although he apologized profusely guaranteeing that it would never happen again, my gut attempted to persuade me otherwise. In the end, his plea for forgiveness convinced me and we buried any memory of the matter. Most of the time he presented an aura of nonchalance and mystery, but from that point on, Marty showed very subtle hints of overprotectiveness.

It didn't take long for a similar event to surface to permanently alter my opinion of him. His parents had a janitorial business, and he helped them out from time to time. Feeling a part of the family, I helped too. We waited until closing time to clean the dentist office. On this day, the last patient happened to be one of our male coworkers, Ben. Ben and I stood in the parking lot and chatted about the workday's events. Marty watched from afar but never came out to join the conversation.

Later that evening when we were alone, he seemed preoccupied. Finally, after a few minutes of silence, he said my smile was too flirtatious. He said that whenever I looked at a man, my eyes invited the man into the bedroom. Therefore, he forbade me to make eye contact with other men. This unreasonable request sought to change the very nature of who I am, but determined to appease my husband, I would honor his request hoping my obedience would make him happy and things better between us.

Without notice, he grabbed one of the industrial mops used to mop the floor, and with all the strength he could muster, hit me across the chest. He hit me again and again as fiercely as he could across my upper body for as long as he could. Screaming from shock and pain, I didn't know if I was imagining a scene from a movie or if this vicious attack was actually taking place. Moments later, after the blueish-purple bruises appeared, I knew that it was real. In the aftermath of the events that night, I realized I had become another statistic.

Every time I replayed the events of that night, fragments of my heart broke. How could someone who supposedly loved me turn into such an untamed animal? The logical answer is that they don't. Love doesn't hurt, or does it? Well, sort of. For two days I didn't communicate with him even though he continuously rang my cell. I needed time to clear my head and think. A range of emotions overwhelmed me. *How could you let this happen? How could you even think about taking him back?* The answer? Love?

I dialed his number and within minutes, he came.

Two years elapsed before we married. At this time, I felt valued and wanted. Like all brides-to-be, the expectation that marriage brings is one of unison and a happily ever after, and things couldn't be better between us. This was the second marriage for both of us, and we had different expectations for our new life together. His expectations seemed simple. Like most men, he wanted my love and attention. However, at twenty-six, my expectations of marriage consisted of more and my determination to make this marriage work took first priority.

For me, my first marriage was a diversion. An escape from the indifferences of my mother. However, life teaches that not all problems require a foreseeable solution. Sometimes, we must be mature enough to wait until the problems dissipate.

Maybe that's why the marriage failed. I watched my older sister run from her problems by getting married in the same way that I was attempting to do. For her, marriage at eighteen proved to be the answer, but we possessed different attitudes about life. Her method of dealing with issues wasn't the same for me. We had two different destinies. However, Aunt Rachel and my sister convinced me that unless London and I got married, we were going to hell and not at a snail's pace either. As I grew older, following Aunt Rachel and my sister's suggestions for my life caused many undesirable consequences.

At first, Marty and my marriage mirrored a television show. The communication, time spent together, and other things were really good. Yet, my "feeler" communicated to me that something wasn't quite right. We began to argue about insignificant things. No marriage is perfect; yet, these arguments felt different.

One day, I opened the door to Marty's car and discovered a half smoked weed cigarette laying in the ashtray. I guess it's true. If you look for trouble, it will find you. My detective skills showcased themselves as I searched the inside of our home. My findings led to a confrontation between Marty and me. He confessed that he sometimes used recreational drugs to make himself feel better. In fact, he needed to feel at ease every time we went somewhere and multiple times throughout the day. Marty's dependence on cannabis became a source of conflict within our marriage. The more I expressed my disapproval with his use, the more contentious he became until finally I surrendered in hopes of making the relationship better.

My acceptance did not make things better, and I struggled to understand why he valued getting high more than he valued our family. Tolerating sin changes our convictions and depletes our beliefs. Before long, liberal thinking dictates acceptance of unsanctioned roads in life. In reality, those roads lead to destruction, but only one leads to heaven. If you travel the road of sin with others, eventually some of the dust will settle on you too.

On occasion we conversed about why he smoked. The idea of who he should be didn't match the reality of who he was. Deep inside, he felt like a failure, so he tried cannabis once. He enjoyed the way it made him feel, so, he made it a habit. It offered an escape from the pressure of his perceived reality and minimized his personal defects. Whenever he smoked, he shared a commonality with others, and they accepted him. Coming down off the euphoria produced by the cannabis made him aware that he must go inside of himself to find acceptance – something he didn't know how to and wasn't willing to do. In reality, he turned his focus to acquiring tangible resources to make him feel better about an imaginary need. Even though his abstract resources provided an unlimited reservoir of potential, he was blinded by his immediate frame of reference. Therefore, his denial of abstract needs precluded moral errors with consequences for everyone.

Marty wasn't like me. He grew up in a two-parent household. *What could have happened to make him view himself this way?* As children, we often test our parents' established boundaries to create a new standard. *Did he push too far? Was he a victim of circumstance or was this taught behavior?* Whatever happened, the hurt made him feel rejected and branded him in a way that evoked strong emotional responses when his needs were not met. These responses crippled him and his relationships.

Before Marty and I got married, I didn't spend a lot of time around his family. As our family expanded, it was only natural that we visited them so that they could bond with their grandchild, Melanie. However, when we did visit, I noticed that Melanie's grandparents often made disparaging remarks about other people. My biggest concern came when they started to undermine my ability as a parent. This behavior weakened my trust in them and damaged my relationship with Marty as well.

Years later, Melanie and her first cousin Emma were in a beauty pageant for the Make-a-Wish foundation. Melanie placed as first alternate in the pageant while Emma did not place at all. Neither Marty's sister nor his parents congratulated Melanie on her accomplishment. Instead, Marty's sister claimed the pageant was rigged in favor of Melanie and stated that she wasn't welcome at her grandparents' home anymore. Their behavior left me speechless! I couldn't believe that they would treat a child that way.

Obviously, I didn't know what I had gotten myself into. People think two parent homes guarantee a solid foundation but this one contained hairline fractures that morphed into gigantic cracks. If my solidarity in the family unit was weakened before, now, it was completely shattered.

Initially, I didn't really notice how much the

race was altering my appearance, but each time that I ran, I began to see changes within me. To be honest, I grappled with a lot of interferences in the race, and a hint of fear grabbed me each time these intrusions showed their faces to me.

As the years rolled by, my husband took his inner frustrations out on the children and me. Why he became angry with me on this day escapes me.

What happened next will always remain etched in my memory. Normally, on Saturdays, we grill for the neighborhood children. JB plays for a travel team, and his coach wanted him to come to the gym and play some pickup games. JB had not done any of his chores, so I said that he couldn't go. Marty became upset because JB couldn't go and began his usual diatribe of calling me out of my name. However, this time, in addition to the name callings and beatings that I received, he spit in my face. I stood there. Motionless and partly numb from disappointment. I knew that I had to be cognizant enough to protect my children, but I never found the courage to fight back though. I simply pleaded with him to stop all the madness.

Marty grabbed his car keys to leave the house

like normal, and I didn't stop him. The rest of us retreated into the house. A couple of hours later Melanie tried to run bathwater for her evening bath. Only problem was that nothing came out. Not knowing what the problem was, I reached for the landline phone to call for help. When I picked up the receiver, I didn't hear the usual dial tone, only complete silence. With no phone nor water, I went to get my car keys. They were gone! Marty had taken them. The children and I were imprisoned at home with no water, no phone, and no transportation. He turned the water off from the main valve outside. I only found this out because in the future when he threw these tantrums, I peered out the window as he left. This became his preferred method of abuse.

Sometimes as you run, pressure builds in the nerves of your feet causing them to go numb. Sin does the same thing to us and only through repentance can we find relief. We must make sure that we adapt to the conditions in life, and faith is the instrumental part. Today, the heat is overwhelming, and it has caused my feet to swell. Heat affects us in different ways - unexpected ways. I stop, momentarily to adjust my shoelaces, hoping this will release the pressure. It's better, but I still feel discomfort.

Marty applied for a part-time job at the local Pizza Pro to reduce the time he spent at home. I was grateful for this job, not because we needed the money, but because Marty seemed more relaxed at home. In fact, Pizza Pro often called him in on scheduled off days. However, when he deposited his check in the bank, the check amount and the supposed hours at work didn't match. Pizza Pro called more often, and he stepped outside to answer the calls. At bedtime, he left his phone face up on the nightstand. The caller id displayed private caller or Pizza Pro. *Wasn't it strange that Pizza Pro called at such inconvenient times?* Asking Marty about the phone calls might not be a good idea, but he is my husband. I have endured unlimited abuse and been faithful to him the whole time. *Shouldn't I know the truth?* Deep down inside, I already knew the answer though.

On rare occasions, Marty and I would just take a drive in the countryside. Later in the evening, we departed for an outing in the car. He gathered his *escape kit* of alcohol and cannabis, and we drove around aimlessly. He needed the escape kit, I guess, to purge his mind of uninvited thoughts. Though, I'm not really sure. Marty climbed into the driver's seat as I hopped in the passenger side. After a few minutes, I mustered up the courage to ask about the secretive phone calls he's been receiving. *Grammy would say anytime they lie to you, they're trying to keep you!* The first time I heard Grammy say this, it didn't make sense. The more I contemplated what she said, I realized that she expressed the truth. If a person's honesty makes you leave, then their lie will make you stay. I wasn't convinced that Marty loved me, but I craved the validation that somehow, he still cared.

As soon as I approached the subject of the secretive phone calls, he became visibly agitated, and stomped heavily on the accelerator. The tire squealed, and my stomach immediately twisted into knots. Petitioning Marty to reduce his speed only increased his agitation. While pleading with God for deliverance, I demanded Marty stop acting foolishly. The more I insisted, the faster he drove. After glancing in his direction, I noticed his eyes were closed. My knuckles nearly burst from clenching the arm rest so tightly while digging my left hand into the seat. If we did wreck, the impact of the collision would be deadly. My God! My God, please help me. Then, without warning, everything stopped as suddenly as it began. Quick, labored breathing interrupted the silence.

Eventually, we made it home. The kids were sleep. For the first time in seven years, my husband truly frightened me. Stifling back tears, I walked slowly to the bathroom and fastened the door. The condemning mirror stood confidently on the wall and beckoned me to come closer. Once there, a disturbed image glared back at me, but I didn't recognize her. Eventually, I determined the damaged woman was me. Years of abuse held my doppelgänger captive, and she embraced it. Now, though, her gripping reality stared me in the face. What she coddled, sickened me. *Why did I accept this behavior?* Mutual respect must abide in a household, and it was evident that our household didn't have that. Clearly, I was a victim of circumstance.

After weeping continuously throughout the night, morning finally came. The consistency of routine re-emerged as the silent predator constantly raped my thoughts. Whispers of sorrow screamed from my heart, but they went unnoticed. Before, I convinced myself that our family life represented the normalcy of others. But now, my intuition worked hard to convince me that change needed to happen. It needed to happen quickly because my life was at risk, and I had grown tired. Tired of pretending. Tired of the hurt and pain. Tired of the abuse. And the demands of life don't stop because I'm nearing exhaustion.

After this epiphany, I nursed my physical and invisible wounds as much as I could. I wanted God to remove me from this situation, but in all honesty, I couldn't see or feel a trace of God anywhere in this area of my life. Things weren't getting better between Marty and me. They were getting worse.

Upon waking up, the day seems exceptionally beautiful despite my circumstances. The birds hum a catchy phrase, and a slight crispness permeates the air. Everyone is sound asleep, and I'm left to enjoy the quietness of morning. My body feels unusually tired though. *It's nothing. Today is a new day.* As I open the refrigerator to prepare breakfast, I glance downward and notice a medium-sized bruise on my leg. *How strange is that?* I don't remember Marty hitting my legs. As I search my mind to determine how I could have gotten the bruise, another one a few centimeters below it, materializes. *That's strange.*

At that moment, my son bounces into the kitchen and invites me to play with him. Out of all things, he wants to ride bikes. Although my energy level is low, I agree to walk with him instead. So, we lace up our shoes and jot outside. JB hops on his bike as I continue to walk. Since we live in a cul-de-sac, it's safe for him to travel ahead of me on the pathway. Although we haven't gotten halfway down the road, I feel faint. Not wanting to set off my son's Spiderman senses, I continue, at a slower pace, as if nothing is wrong. When we make it back to the house, I collapse on the floor for about ten minutes before retiring to the bedroom. Apparently, I look as awful as I feel since Marty peers in my direction without commenting and walks out the door.

Since it's Saturday, rest and relaxation takes precedence. Everything else must wait.

By Monday, my energy reserve is depleted even though I rested all weekend. Still, today is August 27, 2004, a brand new day. I muster the strength to get ready for work. Normally, it's easier to push past the pain but today, I am losing the battle.

After arriving at work, I didn't feel any better. In fact, intense pains began darting through my chest. I told my coworkers Melinda and Tricia about the pain I was feeling. Melinda, being the jokester that she is, told me the pain sounded like gas and to take a tums. I wanted to laugh but the pain from accomplishing such a small feat proved almost impossible.

All at once, I looked upward and noticed that rain clouds began to form. I prayed God would hold back the storm since the race wasn't even near the halfway mark. The clap of thunder indicated a mighty storm was approaching, and the dark gray clouds forged onward. Ulysses had forced me to train in all types of weather. Yet, storms are so unpredictable, and my anxiety kicked in. Interestingly, I learned that every storm contains a bright spot. It's too far to turn back; so, if I fix my thoughts on the bright spot, things won't seem so bad. Afterall, no storm lasts forever. The rain pelted down on my skin as I ran, and at times, I almost lost my footing. Nonetheless, I continued to run with confidence. Then, my perceived limitations began to dissipate.

In agony, I walked to the nurse's station at work. Upon arriving at Nurse Crystal's office, I described my symptoms to her. She said my condition sounded like pleurisy, and she instructed me to take two Ibuprofen. After an hour, I didn't feel better. In fact, I became progressively worse causing Melinda and Tricia concern. They urged me to go see my regular physician. I followed their advice and left. I instinctively called Marty to let him know. Part of me hoped he would meet me there, but without concern, he said ok and hung up the phone.

As I arrived at the urgent care clinic, the pain became more severe. With very little movement, I fill out the required paperwork and wait for the nurse to call my name. I feel weaker. Finally, she calls me to the examination room and jots down my symptoms. The intense pain renders me too weak to verbalize my symptoms. I cry.

Moments later after reviewing my symptoms, the nurse agreed with my work nurse on the original diagnosis of pleurisy. Not accepting the diagnosis, I ask for an x-ray for confirmation. After complying with my wishes, the nurse enters the room seemingly baffled by my x-ray results. She asks if I've ever had pneumonia. I vaguely remember my Aunt Rachel saying I overcame the sickness when I was younger, so I said yes. Becoming a little agitated, I failed to see what this line of questioning had to do with the moment at hand. She took me into a different room that displayed my x-rays and explained that according to her knowledge, my lungs shouldn't be covered with this huge mass. The mass on the x-rays wasn't consistent with pneumonia. *It's funny how the enemy will reveal false evidence to cause fear within.* Ultimately, she stated that Dr. Lee's reading of the x-ray would be final. However, eternity must have passed before he came into the room, but when he did, a rush of emotions overtook me.

Swiftly entering the room, Dr. Lee carried a small piece of crumpled paper in his left hand, and in his right hand, a handful of brochures and began to talk. Consumed by pain, his words are barely decipherable. As his speech continues, fragments of understanding reach me. At some point, a word that ends in -oma demands my attention. I'm not a doctor by any means yet science class taught me that anything ending in -oma means cancerous. Amazingly, the pain that previously held me captive isn't as important as the words coming from Dr. Lee's mouth. *Where is your family? Do they live close by?* And everything else fades into the background.

At twenty-eight years old, the sudden realization of my mortality slapped me in the face. Isolated didn't begin to describe my feelings as Dr. Lee handed me a neatly wrapped death sentence. He emphasized the importance of family, peace, and love in my life right now. *How in the world did I arrive at this point in my life? I'm only twenty-eight years old. Surely this is a mistake, a cruel joke.* Is there really a possibility that I won't live? Lymphoma. Though I've never smoked a day in my life, could this be caused from the years of secondhand smoke from my mother? The battle to understand how I ended up here left me without answers. I peered at the pamphlet. Lymphoma – a blood cancer. There are over seventy different types. Dr. Lee said hopefully I have Hodgkin's lymphoma which is the most treatable type of cancer. Hopefully? *How will I tell my family? How will they react?*

Dr. Lee offered prayers and set up oncology appointments to determine which phase of cancer I had. And just like that, he disappeared. I gathered my belongings, checked out, and walked to my vehicle. To my amazement, the physical pain that I felt moments ago paled in comparison to this emotional roller coaster. Ulysses words are true. Pain lasts as long as you focus on it. Gripping the steering wheel as fiercely as possible, I stared into the horizon with the thought overtaking me. *I'm going to die.*

When I arrived home, Marty was making a sandwich in the kitchen and inquired about my doctor's visit. Without reservation, I told him that I had cancer. His look was one of unbelief. I reiterated the news by showing him the paper with Dr. Lee's diagnosis. He shook his head and walked out the door.

The quietness commanded my thoughts and engulfed the room. My heart believed that deep inside he cared for me. Perhaps, he didn't know how to cope with the information received. Not that I blame him; I didn't know how to cope with it either. I just thought that we could get through it together. Marty didn't come home until after midnight. Because of the circumstances, sleep eluded me. I shared with him that I had a doctor's appointment the next day at the oncology center at 9:00 am. He didn't offer to go with me, so I didn't volunteer any more information.

Marty showed enough reserve to end the physical abuse but continued the verbal abuse. I didn't tell the children about my diagnosis; I didn't want to frighten them without cause. Besides, it's easier to convince myself that everything is alright when fewer people can provide their input.

Whenever Ulysses and I trained, we followed his plan to secure my future as a runner. He called it specificity. Since I had faith in him, I trusted his plan. There were times when his plan seemed tedious and ineffective. So, I tried to improve the process by working when I should have rested. Grammy's voice chimed in. *Remember to rest. You can work Monday through Saturday, but on the Sabbath, take a day to rest.* **Exodus 20:8-10** To my astonishment, the additional exercises proved harmful. Even though I worked with purpose, it wasn't according to Ulysses plan which causes painful setbacks.

I phoned work to let them know about my diagnosis and to discuss a leave of absence to clear my mind. Marty seemed especially agitated with me for some reason, and I tried to avoid him whenever possible. I didn't have the energy – physically or mentally -- to fight with him. But somehow, the fight happened. He began his usual swearing and screaming at the top of his lungs as I stood silently. Angrily, he yelled, "you're always talking about God. So, where's this God of yours now?! Where's this God of yours now that you're sick?" **Psalms 42:3** Then, he walked away and slammed the door behind him.

His words cut to my core because I had become disenchanted by his actions and mockery of my faith. I was angry. Angry at Marty and my situation. I had suffered tremendously due to his constant abuse. *Did I even love him?* It's hard to believe that I fell in love with an illusion and not the true identity of the man I married.

Chapter Three: Mastering the Curve

I know that nothing good comes from anger, but I didn't really know how to feel or what to do. My mind and heart were filled with bleak thoughts, and I needed an effective response to this sickness, this blood cancer. I walked to the bedroom and enclosed myself within the four blue walls to simply be alone. I knelt down beside the bed and began to empty my heart to God. Despair overtook me. Then these words escaped from my mouth. Lord, I cannot fix this burden, and I need your help. You are my source of life, and you can do all things except fail. I wanted to see my children grow old. *What will happen to them? Who will raise them?* My fear isn't dying or pain from this disease but not fulfilling the destiny you have given to me. If you call me home, eternity awaits. If you allow me to stay here, I'll proclaim your goodness to everyone I know the rest of my life. I trust you Lord, and I am ready. Then, I wiped the tears from my eyes, stood up, and waited until the children came home.

From that point on, I lived my life differently. No, I didn't go to the extreme of creating a bucket list filled with adventurous things, but I did go to the extreme of learning to live. Before, I simply existed. Most of all, I wanted to empty myself out when I loved. When the children came home, I enjoyed the moments with them because I didn't get a do-over. Also, I began to work out. My days consisted of hitting the gym in the mornings after the children were in school to calm my mind. I did mostly cardio, but I slowly began to add weights to my training regime. Exercise became my therapy to dismantle most negativity in my life.

At the oncology center, Dr. Crumby asks several questions about my symptoms, and I must admit fear started creeping into my soul. It was something about being in the doctor's office that made all of this so real. So, I did what most people do when they are frightened. I didn't tell Dr. Crumby all of my symptoms hoping that the omission of truth would make this nightmare end. I was losing weight, bruising easily, running fever, and suffering from extreme tiredness. All those things he could see, but somehow, I felt like if I admitted to the night sweats that it made the diagnosis real. Well, this was very real. I can't put into words how out of place I felt each time I came into the oncology center.

On one visit, I saw one of my former classmates.

We weren't really close in high school but when tragedy strikes, people unconsciously bond. Our eyes communicated the uncertainty we each felt because we had been unfairly inducted into this sorority. As Dr. Crumby's nurse scheduled my biopsy for the end of the week, my classmate squeezed my hand to indicate she was both praying and hoping that everything would be alright.

For some reason, Marty began to show me compassion. I guess, maybe, he realized that life is short, and we should treat people like we want them to treat us. So, he decided to join me at my appointment to the urologist. Most of the time, my mom's family would go to the doctor's appointments with me. When they couldn't go, I normally went alone since I didn't know anyone on my father's side of the family. In my heart, I was relieved that Marty decided to go with me. It was a chance for us to bond and hopefully re-establish our relationship. Call me crazy, but sometimes misfortune brings people together. The nurse called my name, and Marty and I walked to the examination room. We were actually having a decent conversation when the doctor walked in.

Dr. Wise greeted us and extended his arm to shake Teri's hand. The only problem is that he thought Marty was Teri. Now, ordinarily this wouldn't have been such a telling moment but the reaction that Marty gave let me know right then, that I was the only one fighting this battle. Marty loudly interjected and said no, no, no. I'm not Teri. She's Teri. And both Dr. Wise and I were a little taken aback. Dr. Wise apologized for the honest mistake. Then, he began asking routine questions to determine what was wrong with me. He had read my chart and discerned my apprehension, so he offered words of encouragement. He said that he just saw a case very similar to mine. Turns out, the guy didn't have cancer. He had an auto-immune disease called sarcoidosis. This gave me a ray of hope even though I didn't know what sarcoidosis was. Anything is better than cancer, right?

After leaving the doctor's appointment, I began to do research on sarcoidosis but there was very little information available. Basically, the research said that sarcoidosis is an autoimmune disease, and it can be fatal. Cancer or sarcoidosis? It didn't help that Bernie Mac, a famous comedian, had just died from complications of sarcoidosis. This sobering fact isn't as reassuring as I thought it could be. *That's enough research for today.* I retired to the bedroom to relax; tomorrow is surgery.

When evening came, the kids took their baths and laid their clothes out for school the next day. Marty came to the bedroom and Melanie, age 2, followed behind him. She jumped into the bed and positioned herself between us like normal. The distance between Marty and I physically was only a couple of inches, but mentally and spiritually, we seemed miles apart. It's hard to bridge the gap when only one person wants to. Marty turned the lights off. As darkness invaded the room, I said a prayer and drifted off to sleep.

While sleeping, I had the most vivid dream I've ever had in my entire life. For miles, all I could see was this endless blinding yellow light. No words can describe the intensity of the light. The oddest thing is that Melanie interrupted my dream as she tossed and turned. After re-adjusting her in the bed, I drifted back to sleep. The dream continued. When I woke up that morning, I knew without reservation that God miraculously healed me! *Jesus healed me!*

The next morning, I got dressed for my scheduled biopsy. The doctor would remove some of the lymph nodes positioned near my lungs to examine them for cancer. Marty drove me to the hospital, and I thought this was a sign that things were getting better between us. I could tell that he was anxious. The side of his mouth turns upward when he's nervous and beads of perspiration form on the center of his forehead. Things were beginning to look up as I carried the healing from my dream in my heart.

After arriving at the hospital, the anesthesiologist sedated me, and I began to drift off into a deep sleep. The only thing I remember her saying is count to ten backwards. *Ten, nine, eight,* ...

The surgery ended and I felt myself coming down from the anesthesia. My eyes slowly opened only to close again. Figures outlined in light blue scrubs and glasses encompassed the room. Distant voices surrounded me, and someone said she's coming to. As this was announced, a male voice whispered, no cancer. Then I closed my eyes and went back to sleep.

The next thing I knew, I was in a recovery room and Marty and my sister were staring me in the face. Marty told me that it was no cancer, and I smiled knowing God fulfilled the promise he had given me. I was healed by His stripes. Isiah 53:5 Thank you, Lord!

After a while, the doctor cleared me to go home.

Once we arrived home, Marty asked if I needed anything as I drifted off to sleep. I awakened to the doorbell ringing. I called for Marty but to no avail. He had gone into Pizza Pro. Sluggishly, I answered the door. My next-door neighbor stood on the other side. She came to check on me and decided that I shouldn't be alone after having surgery. We gathered some of my belongings to spend the night at her house until the anesthesia wore off. Periodically, I woke through the night wondering where I was, but I didn't have the strength to get up. *Maybe it's best that I settle into bed.* I pulled the covers snugly around my body and closed my eyes.

Morning came, and I extended my gratitude for my neighbor's care and concern. However, it was time for me to go home. She voiced concern since Marty wasn't there, but nonetheless, she permitted me to leave. As I walked home, which was less than three minutes away, something about the journey alone seemed rather permanent. Being home alone offered time to reflect about life and changes that needed to occur.

A red light flashed on the telephone; four voice messages were waiting. The doctor's office called about a follow-up appointment, and I now had appointments with a pulmonologist. At my follow up appointment, the doctor diagnosed me with sarcoidosis and told me that the pulmonologist would monitor my lung capacity moving forward. Inwardly, I wasn't satisfied with the diagnosis. I didn't think that Jesus did things halfway. When Jesus heals, he heals completely.

Chapter Four: The Straight away

Accepting a diagnosis of sarcoidosis meant that God didn't heal me completely. As a Christian, God only answers our request with yes, no, and wait. He created the world and me. Surely, he can eradicate this sickness in my body. I believe God and I trust His word.

Before being robbed of my strength, I attended Near the Cross Church in Tupelo, MS. The love of God permeated the church atmosphere. After service, I usually travelled straight home. During an alter call, a gray-haired female standing behind me murmured, "Jesus understands your pain." Inwardly, I marveled at the woman's gall and asked her who did she think she was. Wondering if she was unstable in some way, I simply said, excuse me? She repeated herself. After service, she insisted that I call her. I entered her number in my cell phone but, in all honesty, I was not going to use it. In fact, the whole circumstance surrounding our meeting felt eerie.

Strolling through my phone contacts one afternoon, the strange church lady's phone number appeared. Out of curiosity, I dialed the number, and she answered on the second ring. As we were conversing on the phone, something unexplainable happened. She asked me if I knew a guy named Johnny. I didn't know anyone named Johnny, but she kept inquiring about the guy, and unexpectedly, my doorbell rang. As I opened the door, a man that I didn't recognize stood on the other side. He introduced himself as Johnny and stated he had finished the work Marty hired him to do. Therefore, I went to retrieve my checkbook to pay him for the services.

When the man left, I thought about the events that just transpired. I had never experienced anything like this. How did Mrs. Gore know that this man would be at my house? Feeling my uneasiness through the phone, she simply said, "God showed it to you so no harm would befall you!" While we conversed for several more minutes, she invited me to her house to sit on the porch and listen to the birds. Then, I hung up the phone.

The following Saturday, I visited Mrs. Gore's house to sit on the porch. As we sat, a gentle breeze blew. *We listened as the chimes rendered a beautiful melody, and I took in the ambiance.* At that moment, the wind created a small whirlwind of leaves that caught my attention. I motioned her to look at the whirlwind. She asked me what the whirlwind was saying to me. I thought that was a very odd question and chuckled. *What was it saying to me? Uh, nothing.* Apparently, I must have looked confused. She explained to me how God speaks to us through nature; she said we must seek out the message that our Father is giving to us.

Perplexed, I asked her to explain what she meant even though I thought she may have forgotten her medication. This is a bit strange, but what if there is something to what she's saying. So, I humored her and decided to reflect upon the whirlwind of leaves.

As suddenly as the whirlwind formed, it collapsed. I compared the whirlwind to my cancer diagnosis. I waited in limbo for three months about my health. To me, the three months seemed like an eternity, but in all actuality, the time period was relatively short like the whirlwind. God spoke to me through the whirlwind to let me know that as suddenly as the storm comes with faith it disappears.

Mrs. Gore and I developed a friendship. Actually, to me, it was more than a friendship, maybe even a divine encounter for God to reveal

His purpose for me. She understood me, and most of all, she didn't judge me. She taught me how to be a better person through relying on Christ. She reminded me of my Grammy. Both Mrs. Gore and Grammy said that you have to *confront your problems and deal with your demons. She said that in darkness, sin manifests but in the light, it dries up.* Under her mentoring, I did just that. I began to pray more, and I fasted for the first time.

I didn't know anything at all about fasting, but she taught me. The first time I fasted, I did what you call a Daniel fast for three days. It was hard, but Mrs. Gore told me that denial produces discipline. To me, not eating anything was easier than having to choose what you ate. So, the next time that I fasted, I did a fast with just water. After coming off of the fast, I felt stronger. Certain issues didn't bother me like they did before. I was learning to lay my problems, mainly my marriage, on the alter and not pick them back up.

I discovered Marty cheated on me with one of the cashier's at Pizza Pro. At first, I was hurt and angry, but as time went on, I became less emotional about the infidelity. As a matter of fact, I forgave Marty for everything. It wasn't easy but as I grew in the knowledge of Christ, I understood that when people sin, it's not the people. It is the spirit within them that causes their reaction. With this knowledge, I began to look at Marty differently; I began to look at myself and others differently. I made an effort to look past Marty and see the spirit within. Eventually, I began to really love him. I know that sounds weird, but this love was different from the way that a woman loves her husband. I began to really care for him and his soul. Therefore, whenever, he would try to entice me into an argument, I spoke the written word or kept silent. At first, this annoyed him but eventually, he realized that I was no longer a willing participant in dysfunction. So, he would leave the house and stay gone until all hours of the night. Whenever he left, I prayed. I prayed for him. I prayed for me, and I prayed for the situation. And unspeakable peace followed.

In life, we have freedom of choice, and our path is determined by the choices made. When we chose Christ, the Holy Spirit lives in our hearts and becomes our guide. As he changes our thought process, our actions follow. Under the Holy Spirit's guidance, I found peace. Since relying on His still small voice, circumstances are better. Previously, following the advice of others triggered painful life experiences. Trusting other's ideas for my life's plan resulted in an erroneous purpose, and it offered no comparison to the Holy Spirit's blueprint for my life. God desires to show us our life's design when we trust Him above everything else. Upon entering this race, I exhausted valuable time and energy due to not trusting myself. However, my destination arrival was delayed but certainly not denied.

Trusting yourself and drowning out noise is a prerequisite to victory. Life experiences teach us to trust our inner man. The enemy seeks to destroy our reliance on our inner man by causing confusion to hinder our purpose. Continuously seeking others' advice and never stepping outside of our comfort zones are two ways the enemy undermines our trust. When God said that we should not lean to our own understanding, I got that part right. However, when He gave me a directive, I needed confirmation from other people to affirm my trust in Him.

Of course, in my endeavors, I am incompetent, but when God calls my name, He equips me with the necessary gifts and talents to perform the task. No one can abort the mission he requires us to do except us. When we spend time in prayer with the Father to hear his voice, he reveals the unique path we should travel. Consequently, following anyone other than the Father signifies a lack of faith in Him. Oftentimes, these voices come in different formats from the whisper of a trusted adviser to the attack of an enemy.

For instance, remember when Peter, one of Jesus's trusted friends, tried to hinder Jesus from his mission? Jesus rebuked him. Peter was sincere in his affection for Jesus but his incentive for hindering Jesus's mission was ruled by selfish motivation. Hence, our friends may be sincere in their love for us, but they do not know the Father's intent for our lives. My purpose and my friends' desires may be to sprint in this life's race; however, God may require that I go a steady pace.

Everything happens according to God's timing. When we step outside the sphere of His timing, we become prideful or depressed. Walking ahead of God's plan places Satan on the throne. Walking behind God's plan places ourselves on the throne. We must be in sync with the Holy Spirit, and when we walk in the Spirit, we will not carry out the desires of our flesh. *Galatians 5:15* Meditate on the children of Israel. For each time they listened to the voice of God, expressions of love and provisions rained down. Yet, in their disobedience, pain and defeat were imminent.

God's peace stimulates us to share it with others; so, He led me to start an in-home bible study. We shared our testimonies with others under the leadership of the Holy Spirit. Mrs. Gore taught the study, and I believed many lives were transformed. One Sunday afternoon, my testimony of abuse, registered with a lady named Robin. She pulled me aside and expressed a need for peace. Her voice echoed my previous pain. Initially, she wanted to end her life due to her husband's infidelity. However, through the power of prayer and some counseling sessions, Robin received a breakthrough.

How wonderful to see beautifully broken people healed! Before, experiencing God's goodness, I hid my most painful and hurtful experiences, but God wants us to share our testimonies for His power to be released. When we share our sorrows, our testimony creates hope to overcome the valley. Finally, some beauty from the ashes I had called life.

Your personal transformation and growth may begin to highlight the character of others. For instance, have you ever wondered why people become jealous of your success!? Sometimes, your spiritual growth makes people nervous, and they cast you in a negative light to feel better about themselves. Most people want you to grow, but they don't want you to outgrow them! If your growth surpasses theirs, they may devise plans to limit you. Stand firm.

As I began to submerge myself in God, many attacked my relationship with Him and Mrs. Gore. Some people whom I had always looked up to, tried to bring division between Mrs. Gore and me because they didn't understand the relationship between Mrs. Gore, God, and myself. Nor did they feel a part of my spiritual development. Family spoke negatively about my spirituality due to their own spiritual deficiencies. Negative attitudes and actions of individuals dear to my heart hurt me tremendously because they attempted to obstruct my spiritual progress. In spite of everything, I was maturing, and God himself cradled me in his arms.

The roller coaster ride called life finally began to level out, and life became less chaotic.

The Race Within

Chapter Five: Anchored Through Experience

Without inspiration, nothing begins. Without commitment, transformation never reaches its full potential. Grammy said no one who puts a hand to the plow and looks back is fit for service, **Luke 9:22** and if I commit whatever I'm doing to God, he'll see me through. Looking back, I had the misconception that I needed to be perfect for others to confirm, or to somehow, authenticate my gifts and talents. However, along the way, self-validation and self-worth emerged. Running allowed me to slowly eradicate years of disapproval that had formed within me due to insensitivity, insecurity and ignorance of others and myself.

The presence of these deficiencies guaranteed that I was bound to make wrong choices. By indulging in those choices, the possibility of negatively affecting others existed. I chose to live my life as if it had no value because that's the narrative society communicated to me. Positively influencing my circle hinged upon a complete re-evaluation of my former self since my life was in turmoil. For years, society has taught that having a history, no matter what kind of history it is, dictates value. That's why so many of us with absent parents or no parents at all feel un-loved and under-valued. My fatherless childhood highlighted my low self-esteem among my peers who came from two parent homes. Somehow, society pushed the narrative that a two-parent home, regardless of whether love was present, fostered the myth of self-worth and spiritual grounding. However, spiritual fortification and love must exist within any relational structure to create positivity.

Though some of the lessons have been challenging, this race taught me that pain leads to strength and eventually purpose. When I first started running, it was painful. If a person has ever run before for an extended period of time, most have experienced a soreness in their legs called shin splints that have nearly immobilized them. At certain times, these splints have kept me from achieving goals because I wasn't able to move past the pain of running the race. Most of the time, the hurt that renders us immobilized is deeper than a physical pain. It's a spiritual affliction that manifests itself on an emotional or physical level. I've learned that confronting the issues that cause hurt is the first step to healing. I never imagined that I would experience so much hurt in my lifetime –

molestation, abuse, cancer, rejection, and abandonment.

In fact, often I cried out to God because the pain was so profound. There were many times He didn't answer the way I expected Him to or even thought that I needed him to. Sometimes, I was oblivious to His moving in my situation altogether. He used these times to encourage me and build my faith in him. I was honest with him. I admitted that I couldn't fix the problem on my own. What I've come to realize is that God doesn't want me to fix it at all. He wants my trust. He wants me to trust him completely so I can be an example to others. With all the things that I've gone through, I know because Jesus loves me that whatever I'm going through is the best possible thing that I could go through. I know this because God cares for me, and he is love. He will restore everything that the enemy has taken from me.

Whenever I refuse to address what hurts me, my growth may be stunted or even abnormal causing me to delay or forfeit my full potential. These splints disguise themselves in the form of worry, anger, or fear to render me ineffective, but like all good athletes, when a splint occurs, I need to rest. Therefore, I rest in the arms of my heavenly father.

He is the only one who can ease my pain.

Furthermore, I have often gotten tight hip flexors while I'm running. This pain can be felt all over my body. It represents a lack of courage. To loosen my hip flexors up, I must kneel and stretch. Whenever I kneel to my father and ask for his guidance, I am no longer afraid. He gives me the courage that I need to make it through another day. Oftentimes, his encouraging words stretch my faith in him. It's funny how God will give me an assignment and I feel like I'm going into the situation completely blind. At just the right moment, he will whisper a word of hope and direction to let me know that I'm on the correct path. He doesn't give me a spirit of fear, but one of love, power, and a sound mind to accomplish my purpose. **2 Timothy 1:7**

If you are a believer, God promises to be with you everywhere that you go. I admit that sometimes it's hard for me to trust God in unfamiliar places. This is where my faith must take over. If I say that I am a believer in Christ Jesus, then my belief should be in him. When I kneel to my father in Heaven, my prayer is that he continues to feed me his word and build my faith. The bible tells us that we have to eat his body and drink his blood and though this sounds weird, it is exactly what I desire. **John 6:54** I want the breath of God to overtake me. I want to be so submerged in his Word that I offer my life as a living sacrifice that draws others to God.

There should not be a question as to whether I did anything, but people will know that God did it all through me. Manifesting our dreams and visions is God's desire for us, and I want my life to be that reality. As he told Joshua in the book of Numbers, everywhere that he places his foot, God has given him the land to possess it. Be courageous and believe. That's the same thing God is telling us: continue to study his Word and he will give us the desires of our heart. All throughout the Bible people encountered circumstances that made them fearful. Fear is never a valid reason for disobedience. When we trust God, he will uphold us with his righteous hand. His perfect love dismantles every punishment of fear and strengthens us to the very end.

Now, don't be bamboozled because I haven't always wanted to undertake new challenges, and to be honest, sometimes I am still reluctant. Feeling intimidated is natural due to our humanity. However, we must not let the fear take residence or precedence in our life. The indwelling spirit of God diminishes that fear if we submit to Him. In times past, the uneasiness of trying something new nearly overwhelmed me and paranoia and uncertainty attempted to hold my soul captive. I felt like people watched to see if I would fail or tried to deliberately set me up. This feeling made me nervous. God *said that we shouldn't be anxious for anything but in everything, by prayer and supplication, with thanksgiving, let our requests be made known to God.* **Philippians 4:6** God made known to me the intent of this verse through the trials in my life. Many times, I would wish for certain circumstances to change. I have learned to be patient because God is working out my soul's salvation in the process even though it may feel uncomfortable.

For instance, as a teacher, it is my responsibility to impart knowledge within my students for their success. Jesus does the same thing for us when we allow him. He is always willing to teach us everything we need to know. We are to desire the pure milk of the word to grow into the full experience of salvation that we may be disciples of Christ. Partaking of a diluted version of his word fills us for a short time only to leave us lost. For instance, my students must learn the parts of speech to write an effective sentence. If they do not master the parts of a sentence, their communication will be incomprehensible.

As the teacher, I must exhibit genuine care for their willingness to learn while not scolding them for a lack of knowledge. I must create an atmosphere conducive to learning and free of criticism, and that's what Jesus does for us. When we desire and ask of him, he freely gives without reservation because he loves us. There is no condemnation for the things that we have done. His attitude is genuine love. God's lessons are intentional and so is God's discipline. When we don't want to do things God's way, we grieve the Holy Spirit, and give Satan a chance to rule in our lives. As I become more comfortable with yielding myself to the ultimate trainer, my pains go away. I am no longer a slave to toxic ideas or resistance to change because I know that the person orchestrating the change is in full control and has a plan that will not harm me.

During my training, some of my fellow athletes were plagued by runner's knee or stiff knee. In the spiritual realm, this affliction suggests a hint of pride or an inability to humble yourself. But what exactly is pride? Independence and rebellion? Scripture says pride goes before a fall. An attitude of pride is associated with an excessive amount of self-worth since worthiness originates in Jesus. Anytime we desire self-will above God's will, we exhibit pride and are doomed to hell if we continue down the destructive path. We face the risk of becoming egotistical and edging God out.

Sometimes pride can be difficult to recognize because it manifests itself so differently. Pride can be boisterous and obnoxious, but it can also be in the form of shyness. When I was younger, I characterized myself as extremely shy. I was very reserved. As I searched deeper to discover who I am, I realized that my shyness was rooted in the fact that I wanted the approval of my parents as if God's approval wasn't good enough.

In talking to God, he convinced me that if no one ever noticed me, that he does. He sees everything that I do. He knew me before I was knit in the darkness of my mother's womb. In fact, we were created in darkness for the purpose of His light and truth. Therefore, our mission should be to bring honor to his name even when others cannot recognize our worth. Are you guilty of exhibiting hidden pride? A prideful attitude may indicate that we are not mature enough to walk in obedience with our Lord.

The most common injury that I suffered from during training was stress fractures which are microscopic tears from overuse. When diagnosed with stress fractures, they are usually a surprise for me. Sure, I felt discomfort, but the old saying goes, no pain no gain, right? I have always been taught to push past the pain, but pushing past the pain can lead to repetitive trauma.

Sometimes, we repeatedly subject ourselves to emotional trauma because we think the outcome will be different. God wants us to know that we should not delay in dealing with hurt. I had a dream that my ring finger had been cut. The severity of pain was so intense that I awoke from my dream to actually examine my finger. While examining my ring finger, I noticed an indentation that mimicked the cut, and I caressed it for several minutes before falling back to sleep. When I awoke after a couple of hours, the indentation was gone. God revealed to me that even though I had forgiven my ex-husband for the abuse, I had not forgiven myself. Because of the guilt and shame that I felt, I often replayed the incidents in my mind. Unforgiveness in any form is not good because it tries to abort God's purpose for your life by immobilizing you. Not only had I not forgiven myself, but I didn't fully realize the extent of my ignorance. Living with the hurt kept me from walking in the full potential of my gift. Spiritual hurt always manifests itself physically, and fortunately, God spoke to me through a dream so that I could seek his healing from the internal wounds.

The motivation to attempt an endeavor begins in the mind, and it must be superseded by action. However, we should take action in accordance to God's will. The old adage says that talk is of little value. However, we know that is not true since life and death literally lie in the power of the tongue. When God speaks, he is the voice of authority. Since you and I are made in his image, we possess that same authority. *As his mouthpieces, we must be eager to speak His truth so that our belly is satisfied.* **Proverb 18:20** When we speak truth, our lips produce fruit. The word tells us that *out of his belly shall flow rivers of living water.* **John 7:38** and **Revelations 21:6** confirms that Jesus is Alpha and Omega the beginning and the end. To the thirsty, he promises to give from the spring of the water of life without payment. Yet, it is not enough to merely speak God's word, we must be eager to perform the task that God has set before us.

I have learned that perfection is not attainable in

human effort alone and that is perfectly OK. When I was in grade school, I made straight As, had "perfect" attendance, and was the epitome of the teacher's pet. After a year in college, one of those characteristics didn't describe me anymore. I was on the verge of not being an all A student! Because of this "perceived" failure, I withdrew. Yes, that's right! I withdrew from what I perceived as a difficult class and from college altogether. I had never made anything less than an A, and it terrified me. Most people strive for perfection because they are afraid of failure. However, failure is a necessary part of success. Sometimes, people do not recover from failure due to fear. Fear is a crippling emotion that can be fatal when a lack of spiritual awareness exist. However, God never gave us a spirit of fear, so we don't have to be subjected to it.

Remember when David volunteered to fight Goliath? Because of his age, many considered him too young for the military and not qualified. As a matter of fact, he was only a teenager when he answered the plea to fight. Saul offered David his armor to fight with, but David refused it because it was too big for him. His refusal of the outward armor only highlighted his inward reliance on our Savior. David possessed the right attitude towards the battle. He had a clear vision of what he could accomplish, and he won the fight with tools designed for him by God. When I do not operate in my own gifts, I am not as effective as I should be. I am also being disobedient. In essence, I am telling God that he made a mistake in his design of me. I never thought I would tell God that! No matter what challenges life offers, as believers, everything needed to overcome them is within us.

Can you imagine telling the creator of the world that He is insufficient? That's exactly what I did when I tried to operate in gifts and talents that He didn't give me. For a long time, I lived as an imposter, and God doesn't like imposters. Not only did I deceive others, but I deceived myself. I didn't try to be deceptive, but I adopted this imposter syndrome based on my interactions with others. I became an imposter due to fear. Fear of not being accepted by people who were supposed to love me. God would later reveal that the people who didn't accept me were not meant to be lasting characters in my story. In fact, some of the characters were villains who helped me see the beauty in ashes. My ashes were the imperfections that God used to make me whole. He perfectly designed my defects to highlight the restoration process he would take me through. That restoration process involves shining the light on our imperfections so that God can attain the glory. Everyone has hidden flaws that foster guilt or shame. But when God shines His light, the restoration process can begin. When we reject that process, we place our soul and the souls he ordained us to touch in jeopardy.

Another lesson revealed is that comparison of yourself to others is harmful. As I began to have a relationship with my earthly father, he told me that I should never compare but learn to identify. At first, I didn't know the difference between the two. Webster's defines the word compare as measuring or evaluating two seemingly like things. To identify something means there is recognition of what something is. The difference of the two is that identifying something requires understanding and promotes discovery. Comparing something implies that the full knowledge of understanding hasn't been established. When I identify, I can recognize my worth, but when I compare myself to others, my worth is not known. The tendency to compare ourselves to others causes division. We experience feelings of inadequacy and the comparison indicates that a true understanding of God escapes us. If we don't have any understanding of who our savior is, how strong are we in the faith? Remember people perish for a lack of knowledge, and what good is knowledge without understanding? Rejecting the knowledge of God means that He will reject us as his priests. ***Hosea 4:6*** We must trust God above anyone else, and when we compare ourselves to others, we do not believe God since we continue to search for something he has already declared. To be willing to trust man above God renders our reliance upon Him worthless. If our desire is stronger to trust man, then are we really servants of Christ? Joshua told the Israelites they must choose who they will serve, and the same is true for us.

There have been times when I wanted man's acceptance, but man's acceptance means denying God. Jesus says that whoever denies him on earth, he will also deny them before his father in heaven! Ask yourself does fear of man keep you from obedience. Are you always searching for confirmation? If the answer is yes, then a problem comparing may exist. It robs you of confidence and faith; we know it is impossible to please God without faith. Therefore, we must rightly evaluate the word of God so it can accomplish its purpose in our life.

Success is not solitary. In life, we need people

to support us. The hardest thing to do is go through life alone. I know as a Christian that we are never alone, but I mean naturally speaking. God created us to be in community with others. When I was diagnosed with cancer, my ex-husband and I were in a bad place and there was no support offered from him. This lack of support crippled me, and it impaired my ability to trust others. As a matter of fact, God showed me on several occasions that I needed to deal with the spirit of abandonment and rejection. When a person's feels abandoned or rejected, feelings of perfectionism, pride, inferiority, and fear among other things take root in his or her life. I felt abandoned at an early age, actually all throughout my life until I cried out to Jesus to meet my need and accepted His help. The deliverance happened overnight, but the healing became a process.

Sometimes, I would ask God why? I remember asking God several times, why wasn't I good enough. My father abandoned me. Even though I knew my mom, she didn't raise me. My husband abused me. I was never angry with God, but I did want to know why.

Who told you that was his response? It is easy to hear the voice of man, and when we listen to those voices, we begin to question God's voice and his authority which leads to sin. God taught me that the "why" isn't important but trusting Him completely is. He wanted to know if I would trust him to deliver me from my circumstances. Later, God revealed to me that he would indeed deliver me! Hallelujah.

Is there anything worse than running with nowhere to go? Run with purpose. The Bible tells us that people perish for lack of vision. The vision God chooses for an individual's life will be specific to His needs and purpose. It will not be a complicated design. God says in **Habakkuk 2:2-3** *to write the vision, make it plain on tablets, so he may run who reads it. For still the vision awaits its appointed time; it hastens to the end – it will not lie.* If it seems slow, wait for it, it will surely come, it will not delay. As human beings, we do not always agree with God's timing or his plan for our life due to self-seeking intentions, but His timing is always perfect.

There is often a craving to "get there" quicker by traveling a different path. However, we must realize that God is omniscient, and his plan is to make our paths straight. Because we are limited in knowledge, sometimes God's plan doesn't seem like it makes sense. In all honesty, sometimes it's almost unbelievable. If God really told us the path for our life, would we believe him? That is why we must walk by faith and allow God to direct our path. God never shows us the finished path design for our lives. He takes us through each nuance of the trail to increase our reliance in Him. God wants us to know that he is our first love, and as our first love, nothing else compares to him.

This is why we should not be anxious in our efforts but trust God to lead us along the way. When we wander outside the boundaries of his grace, He waits patiently for us to return. Due to his love, we are able to extend that love to others and to walk in the beauty that he models for us. God so loved the world that he gave his only begotten son that whosoever believes in him should not perish but have everlasting life. God sent Jesus into the world not to condemn it but that through him the world might be saved. **John 3:16-17** As representatives of Christ we must model that same love to our brothers and sisters. God modeled this behavior to us as an example to draw others to Him. We were filthy sinners; yet, His love saved us. Therefore, as ambassadors for Christ, we must look past our brethren's flaws because love covers a multitude of sin.

Gradually, I discovered that I could begin to create my own history by following a different story – his story. Using his story, I inherited an identification that society wanted to hide and steal from me. The identification of a black woman. As a person of color society tends to rewrite our history to make it more comfortable for them. When they do that it takes away from who we are as a people and minimizes our contribution to society. When anyone is stripped of his or her contributions to society, a tendency to revert back to the narrative that other people have written for us. In reverting back, we invalidate the path that God has chosen for us. If it's written in God's word that we should not lean to our own understanding, why would we allow ourselves to adopt the understanding of others? People will label you based on their insecurities when they operate in an unauthentic version of themselves while aborting not only their dreams but the dreams of others. Do not accept their narrative for your life. You are destined for greatness because the Great I AM declared it.

Determine whether you are sprinting or running a marathon. In life, you will encounter both so therefore train with intensity. Impediments will happen daily, but as I continue to run, the setbacks morph into opportunities for the next competition. The race is not to the swift or the battle to the strong, but time and chance will tell the outcome. **Ecclesiastes 9:11** Valuable things are formed slowly and with pressure, and we are no different. God is faithful and we will receive His promises.

The best part about my race is that I become more intimate with Jesus. Now, when I encounter runner's interference, I pray and listen to what Jesus is trying to tell me. Sometimes, it's hard to drown out the noise of other people's advice or the conflicting moments, but it must be done. I must go to the secret place and be alone with my father. God promises to give me peace that surpasses all understanding. He won't let me fight alone unless I choose to since He doesn't infringe on my will. The gigantic mountain for me is merely God's little incline. In fact, that little incline is a learning opportunity that Jesus uses to teach me. If the moment is painful, he alters my attitude to reveal the purpose behind the pain that I suffer. If it is a happy moment, He lets me know that he is my pleasure and as my first love, he desires to see me fulfilled.

The Race Within

Epilogue/Conclusion

Life is composed of a series of sprints and marathons that make up a person's journey. One day, the journey will come to an end and the marathon will be complete. Until that day comes, run with the same intensity and passion as when you started. As I've grown older, my purpose for running changed, and I no longer experience the need to enter competitive races. Sometimes I sprint and other times, I take long leisurely runs on a pathway of God's choosing.

The Race Within

Acknowledgement

First and foremost, I would like to thank Jesus Christ because without Him none of this would be possible. He is my source for living. Also, I want to thank my parents for teaching me how to rely on my inner strength which is God. Thank you to Herticine Goree for feeding me the word of God and showing me how to really love people in spite of their actions towards you.

Thank you to my parents, grandparents, and "Marty" for shaping my life in different ways to make me who I am today. I also extend my gratitude to special friends for listening, encouraging, and having faith in me to write this book. Lastly, to all the characters within my life that helped me to develop the plot in which I call my life story. May God richly bless everyone who reads this book and those who contributed in some manner.

The Race Within

About The Author

The author is the divorced mother of three beautiful children and grandmother to one grandson. She is a graduate of Blue Mountain College in Blue Mountain, MS where she received a dual degree in English and Education. She currently resides in Tupelo, MS. Her hobbies include lifting weights, writing, and spending time with family.

The Race Within